Rick's
# #
Eleven
Song Book

Lyrics
&
Scores
By
Richard Mousseau

MOOSE HIDE BOOKS
imprint of
MOOSE ENTERPRISE PUBLISHING
PRINCE TOWNSHIP
ONTARIO, CANADA

cover illustration by Rick Mousseau

Rick's # Eleven Song Book
Copyright March 1, 2024
Richard Mousseau

Published March 1, 2024
by

MOOSE HIDE BOOKS
imprint of
MOOSE ENTERPRISE PUBLISHING
684 WALLS ROAD
PRINCE TOWNSHIP
ONTARIO, CANADA
P6A 6K4
web site www.moosehidebooks.com

NO VENTURE UNATTAINABLE

CREATED IN CANADA

Library and Archives Canada Cataloguing in Publication

Includes Index.
Issued in print and electronic formats.

Mousseau, Richard 1953- Author of Lyrics and Musical Scores
Rick's # Eleven Song Book / Richard Edmond Mousseau

Issued in print and pdf formats
ISBN 978-1-927393-79-6(pbk.). - -ISBN 978-1-927393-80-2(pdf)

TABLE OF CONTENTS

PAGE# TITLE

Rick's
# #
Eleven
Song Book

A Chance With Romance

Lyrics by
Richard Mousseau

Score by
Richard Mousseau

=80 Pop
Intro
G Am G
V 1
Some-where
7
D G
there is some - one wait-ing for some - one like me, need-ing some - one
12
Em D G D Am
Chorus
like you to fall in love with some-one like me. Lone-ly hearts crave the
17
D G Em D
ess-ence of a ten - der em - brace. Lone-ly hearts seek true love from a
22
G Am G
Bridge
hope - ful chase for a chance with ro - mance.
28
D G Em D
34
G D Am D
Chorus
Lone-ly hearts crave the ess-ence of a ten - der em -

684 Walls Rd. Prince Twp., Ontario Canada P6A 6K4
mooseenterprises@on.aibn.com www.moosehidebooks.com

39 G Em D G Am 2
brace. Lone-ly hearts seek true love from a hope - ful chase for a
44 G V 1
chance with ro - mance. Some - where there is some - one wait-ing for
49 D G Em D
some - one like me, need-ing some - one like you to fall in love
54 G D G End Am
with some-one like me. With hope for a chance with ro -
59 G Am G
mance

A Hint Of Romance

Lyrics by
Richard Mousseau

Score by
Richard Mousseau

♩=92 Pop /Easy Listening
Intro
F C G
Am C G C
V 1
Sail a-way with me on a south wind.
G Am
let the sum-mer sun warm your heart where the oc - ean waves rock us to sleep.
C G C
V 2
Don't let your wor - ries keep us a-part. Walk u-pon sand so warm to the touch.
G Am
Let your cares float a - way on a breeze. un - der the stars at night walk with me,
C G C
Chorus
F C
and let my love be - gin to tease. Sweet mu - sic drifts past as we dance. We
G Am C G C
smile a smile, may-be a kiss by chance. By chance a hint of ro - mance.

684 Walls Rd. Prince Twp., Ontario Canada P6A 6K4
mooseenterprises@on.aibn.com www.moosehidebooks.com

34
2
Bridge
F C G Am
40
C G C
V 3
It's so darn cold up in this North-land. I just don't know
45
G Am C
why we stay here. Sail a-way with me to a trop-ic isle where we will be warm
49
G C
V 2
most of the year. Walk u-pon sand so warm to the touch. Let your cares float a -
53
G Am C G C
way on a breeze. un-der the stars at night walk with me, and let my love be - gin to tease.
58
Chorus
F C G
Sweet mu - sic drifts past as we dance. We smile a smile, may-be a kiss by
63
Am C G C
Chorus
F
chance. By chance a hint of ro - mance. Sweet mu - sic drifts past as we
68
C G
dance. We smile a smile, may - be a kiss by

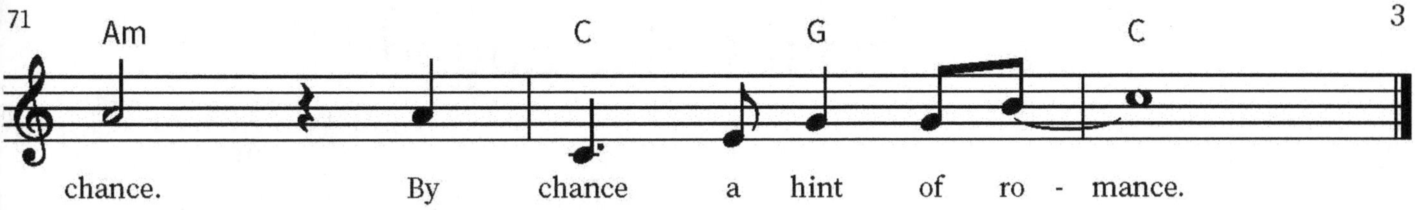
71
3
Am
C
G
C
chance. By chance a hint of ro - mance.

A Rumour Going Round

Lyrics by
Richard Mousseau

Score by
Richard Mousseau

=126 Country Rock
Intro
Em C
Am G V 1
They thought I was the star of a
D C
rock and roll show. For the gals in town I was damn good all know. All
G D C
through the night they were knock-ing on my door. A ru-mour go - ing round some -
G Em C
one swore - . I was the lead sing-er seek - ing an ea - sy la - y with the
Am D Em
lo - cal girls who are al-ways will-ing to play. It's cr - zy to think, but ea-sy to sc-
C Am D G
ore when they think I'm the star they a - dore.

684 Walls Rd. Prince Twp., Ontario Canada P6A 6K4
mooseenterprises@on.aibn.com www.moosehidebooks.com

31
2
V 2
I was seen in the arms of a well known la - dy but the truth be told the
35
D C G D
facts were sha - dy. The lo - cal boys they were knock-ing down doors. The
39
C G Em
ru-mour go-ing round some-one swore - . I was the lead sing-er seek-
43
C Am
ing an ea - sy la - y with the lo - cal girls who are al-ways will-ing to
47
D Em C Am
play. It's cr - zy to think, but ea-sy to sc - ore when they think I'm the
52
D G Em
Bridge
star they a - dore.
57
C Am D
62
Em C Am D

67
G
3
V 3
When my ruse is done I'll
71
D
C
head out of town and the star of the show will have an odd frown when the
75
G
D
C
G
lo - cal boys go knock-ing on his door. The ru-mour go-ing round some - one swore -
79
Em
C
. He said, "It was-n't him and this hap-pened be - fore. There's a
83
Am
D
Em
guy who looks like me and he's out to score. It's ca - zy to think, but ea - sy to
88
C
Am
D
G
see, my twin broth-er he looks just like me."
93
C
End
G
A ru-mour go-ing round some - one swore - . I was the
97
Em
C
Am
lead sing-er seek - ing an ea - sy la - y with the lo - cal girls who are

101
D
Em
C
4
al-ways will-ing to play. It's cr - zy to think, but ea-sy to sc - ore when they
106
Am
D
G
Em
think I'm the star they a - dore. It's cr - zy to think, but ea-sy to sc -
111
C
Am
D
ore when they think I'm the star they a -
114
G
Em
C
dore.

An Afternoon On A Blustery Christmas Eve

Lyrics by
Richard Mousseau

Score by
Richard Mousseau

=108 Christmas
Intro
He
D
V1
G
came in-to my bar down - heart-ed it seem-ed. It was just an after-noon on a
Am
D
G
blust-ery Christ-mas Eve. His eyes on-ce bright, I say no-long-er gleam-ed. He
Am
D
G
had a ha-rd year and he came in here to grieve. He slump-ed on a stool, his
Am
D
G
eyes red from tears. I heard him say I've had bet - ter years. Do you
Am
D
see this list and I've check-ed it twice. Of all these names not one has been
G
Em
Chorus
D
G
nice. I asked would you care for your u-sual? He said, 'if it's not too much

684 Walls Rd. Prince Twp., Ontario Canada P6A 6K4
mooseenterprises@on.aibn.com www.moosehidebooks.com

33
Am D G Em Am D
2
troub-le I'd like a doub-le.' I brew-ed hot co-co with a shot of map-le syr-up his
37
Em Am D
ri-tual on Christ-mas eve. The
42
D G
V2
coat that he wore had seen bet - ter days. He sip-ped hot co - co and he
46
Am D G
slow-ly be-gan to glow. I was at odds at what I should say as he
51
Am D G
check-ed off names he sud-denly said Ho Ho. His eyes scan-ned the list as a
55
Am D G
slight smile - grew. His cheeks grew red-der and sud-denly I knew. His
60
Am
list of naugh-ty names sud-denly changed to nice. He said it's al-ways wize to
64
D G D G
Bridge
check San-ta's list twice.

3
69 D D V3 G
He came in-to my bar down - heart-ed it seem-ed. It was
73 Am D
just an after-noon on a blust-ery Christ-mas Eve. But be-fore he left his eyes they did
78 G Am D
gleam. His list of names no - long-er made him grieve. He
82 G Am
grabbed his bag of gifts just for girls and boys. For the child-ren of the world he
86 D G
had plen-ty of toys. Each year the naugh-ty list San-ta will al-ways check
90 Am D G
twice. And be - fore he leaves the child-ren are all nice. I
94 Em Chorus D G Am
asked would you care for your u-sual? He said, 'if it's not too much troub-le I'd like a
98 D G Em Am D
doub-le.' I brew-ed hot co - co with a shot of map-le syr-up his

101
Em
Am
D
4
ri-tual on Christ-mas eve.

Behind A Window Shade

Lyrics by
Richard Mousseau

Score by
Richard Mousseau

♩= 112 Pop Rock
Intro
G Em G Em
From my win-
V 1
G Am
dow I wat-ched the night come a - live. Brook-lyn a-part-ments hide the sun af-ter
G Em G
five. Ba-bies cry a-bove the rum-ble of the high-line train. The sum-mer heat all
Am G Em G
V 2
day and night, the clouds they hold no rain. From a win - dow a man he
Am G
plays a sooth-ing sax. Brook-lyn ten-ants soon be-gin to re - lax. Moth-er's
Em G Am
call, it's time to feed their hun-gry brood. A couple I see a - cross the way, are
G Em Am D G
Chorus
in a ro-man-tic mood. I watched sha - dows be-hind a win-dow shade. Ro -

684 Walls Rd. Prince Twp., Ontario Canada P6A 6K4
mooseenterprises@on.aibn.com www.moosehidebooks.com

2
36 C F G Em Am D G
mance to-night may have a chance, as they dance be-hind a win-dow shade.
41 Em Am D G C F G
Bridge
46 Em Am D G Em G
V 3
In the heat of the night peop-le
51 Am G
sleep on their bal - co - ny. Brook-lyn's lone-ly hearts seek com-pan - y. Old folks
56 Em G
sit to talk and sip the wine of youth. All eyes will watch the
60 Am G Em
win-dow with the shade pulled down, yes that's the truth. A lone
64 G Am
V 4
voice of an an - gel sings a sooth-ing rhyme. Brook-lyn ten-ants soon sway in
69 G Em G
time. Ba-bies sleep, as the stars a - bove light up the sky. Be - hind a shade two

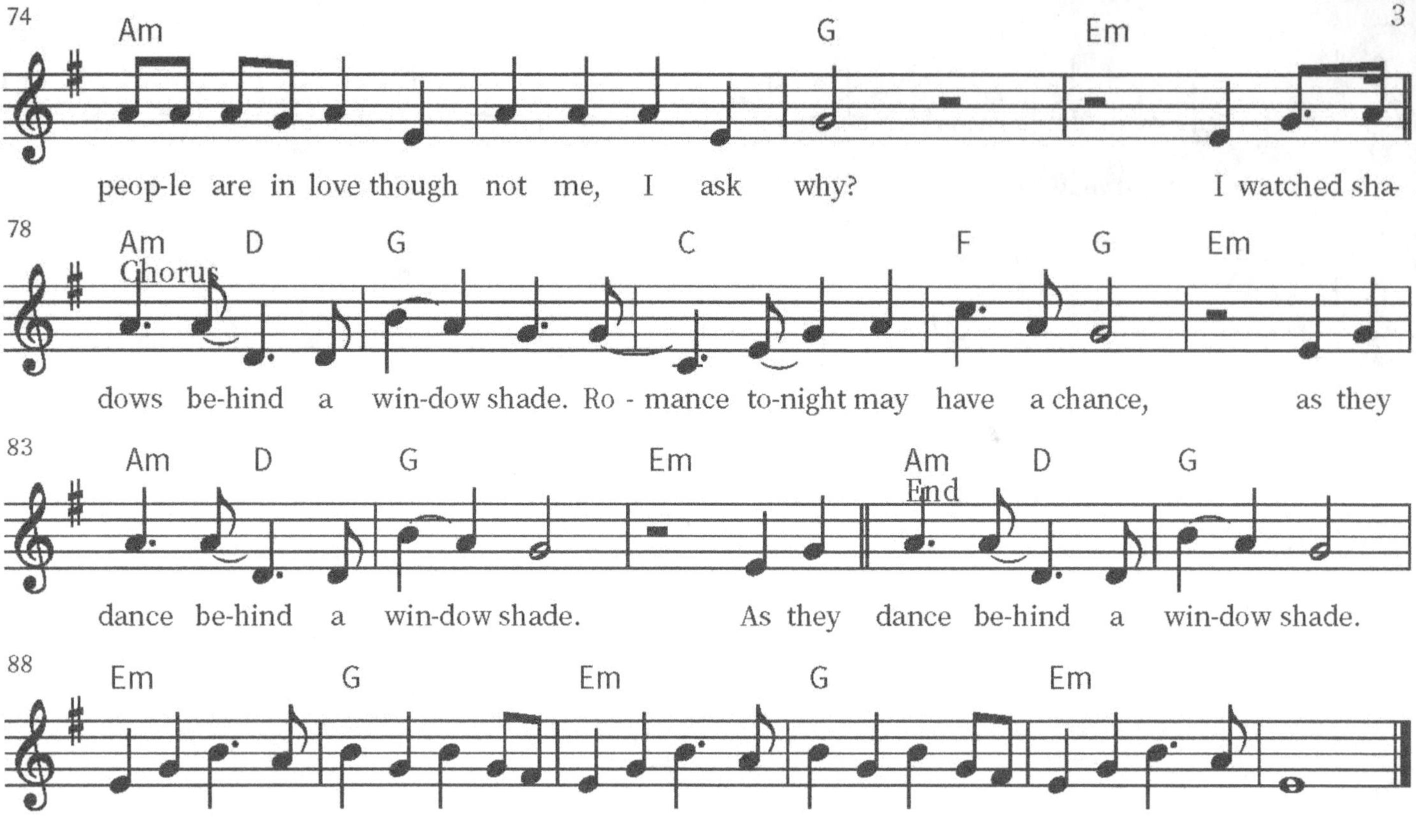
74
Am G Em
3
peop-le are in love though not me, I ask why? I watched sha-
78
Am D G C F G Em
Chorus
dows be-hind a win-dow shade. Ro - mance to-night may have a chance, as they
83
Am D G Em Am D G
End
dance be-hind a win-dow shade. As they dance be-hind a win-dow shade.
88
Em G Em G Em

Bitter Sweet

Lyrics by
Richard Mousseau

Score by
Richard Mousseau

♩=112 Celtic
Intro
F C F Bb
V 1
He came through the mist from a schoon-er up-on the
7
C F Bb C
sea. A Buc - can-eer I'm told who charm-ed young An - nie May. A -
12
Am G C F Bb
lone on the sea-side cliff she is heard to de - cree, a love for a scoun - drel she
17
C F C F Bb
Chorus
met on Bon - ny Bay. Bit - ter sweet was her life up-on the
22
Am C F Bb
cliffs of Bon - ny Bay where winds cut like a knife. A whisp-er is heard to
27
C F Bb C
say, she waits on the cliff each night in - to the mist to cast a light.
32
F Bb Am C F
V 2
Bit - ter sweet so they say was the life of An - nie May. He walks through the

684 Walls Rd. Prince Twp., Ontario Canada P6A 6K4
mooseenterprises@on.aibn.com www.moosehidebooks.com

37
Bb C F
2
moss up-on the cliffs of Bon-ny Bay. A child of six I'm told who
42
Bb C Am G C
wand-ers a-bout care-free. Be-fore the ru-mours start what must she say. She
47
F Bb C F C
tells him stor-ies true of a sail-or who sails the seas.
52
F Bb Am C F
Bridge
V 3
He came through the
57
Bb C F
mist from a schoon-er up-on the sea. An old man I'm told he was in
62
Bb C Am G C
search of An-nie May. Through the dark of night a light he could see and
67
F Bb C F C
hopes his love waits up-on the cliffs of Bo-ny Bay. I
72
F Bb C F
V 4
walk through the moss up-on the cliffs of Bon-ny Bay. An old man now I

77
Bb C Am
3
am who knows the true folk - lore of the sail-or from the sea and the
81
G C F Bb C
loves of An - nie May. The end-ing of my tale I'll leave to folk -
86
F C F Bb Am C
Chorus
lore. Bit-ter sweet was her life up-on the cliffs of Bon-ny Bay where
92
F Bb C
winds cut like a knife. A whisp-er is heard to say, she
96
F Bb C F
waits on the cliff each night in - to the mist to cast a light. Bit-ter sweet so they
101
Bb Am C F
End
say was the life of An - nie May. Bit - ter sweet so they
105
Bb Am C F C
say was the life of An - nie May.

Bring Your Love Home To Me

Lyrics by
Richard Mousseau

Score by
Richard Mousseau

684 Walls Rd. Prince Twp., Ontario Canada P6A 6K4
mooseenterprises@on.aibn.com www.moosehidebooks.com

32
C
G
V 2
2
bring it on home to - me.
I bust my back to pay the rent,
36
Am
C
D
and you find ways to spend each cent. I won-der what's on your mind. If
40
G
it's a man you want to find then bring it on home bring your love,
44
C
G
Bridge
bring it on home to - me.
49
C
C7
C
54
Em
D
G
59
C
G
V 3
If you real-ly want to cheat on me
64
Am
C
D
then tell me that's the way it will be but if you want to change your mind, and

68
G
I'm the man you want to find then bring it on home bring your love,
72
C
G
Chorus
bring it on home to - me. Yes bring it on home, bring your love,
76
C
bring it on home to - me. Do you know you cause me stress, so
80
C7 C Em D
ba-by I must con - fess. if you have a night-out plan, but real-ly care a-bout your
85
G
man, then bring it on home bring your love, home to -
89
C G
End
C
me.

Coconut Bay

Lyrics by
Richard Mousseau

Score by
Richard Mousseau

♩= 108 Soft Rock
Intro
A E6 A E
On the
V 1
F♯m B7 E
lee-ward side of our is-land, a salt breeze sways the co-co-nut trees. In the
D E F♯m B7 E
bay I swim with an is-land maid-en and dine and sip sweet co-co-nut wine. This
F♯m B7 E
night be-neath the stars we slow dance, our hearts filled with ro - mance. In my
D E F♯m B7 E E6 E
Chorus
arms I hold my is-land maid-en and pray to re-turn to Co-co-nut Bay. On our
A E D G
is-land un-der a mis-ty moon - light we walk on shift-ing sands with de -
F♯m B7 E D E
light. A warm sea breeze sets us in a trance for lov - ers to find

33
2
E6 A E E6 E A
Bridge
true ro - mance.
39
E D G F♯m B7
44
E D E E6 A E
50
F♯m B7 E
V 2
I set sail from our is - land a salt breeze fills our sails to the keys. In my
54
D E F♯m B7 E
dreams I hold my is - land maid- en and kiss sweet lips of the gal I will miss. On the
58
F♯m B7 E
Sloop John - B I am Cap- tain, a salt breeze fills our sails on the seas. In my
62
D E F♯m B7 E E6 E
Chorus
dreams I hold my is-land maid-en and pray to re-turn to Co-co-nut Bay. On our
67
A E D G
is - land un - der a mis - ty moon - light we walk on shift-ing sands with de -

72
F♯m B7 E D E
3
light. A warm sea breeze sets us in a trance for lov - ers to find
77
E6 A E D
End
true ro - mance. For love - ers to
81
E E6 A Nc A E
find true ro - mance, on Co-co-nut Bay.

December Morning

Lyrics by
Richard Mousseau

Score by
Richard Mousseau

♩=104 Folk Rock
Intro
Em A F♯m D
6
V 1
Em A
It's damn cold - this De-cem-ber morn-ing on a wind-y street head-ing
11
D G Em
no-where. It's damn cold - yet I will keep on walk-ing in
15
A D G D
Chorus
search of a life and love that I can share. Love is con - fu-sion and il - lu-sions. My
20
A D Em
lone - ly heart has no home. On a cold De-cem - ber morn-ing these
24
A F♯m D Em
V 2
emp - ty streets I roam. I'm damn lone-ly this De-cem-ber morn-ing. Her
29
A D
name was Anne and our love was once bit - ter sweet. I re - call - her

684 Walls Rd. Prince Twp., Ontario Canada P6A 6K4
mooseenterprises@on.aibn.com www.moosehidebooks.com

33 G Em A 2
words u-pon my leav-ing. 'I hope you find a love that you can
37 D G Chorus D A D
share. Love is con-fu-sion and il-lu-sions. My lone-ly heart has no home. On a
42 Em A F♯m D G Bridge
cold De-cem-ber morn-ing these emp-ty streets I roam.
47 D A D Em
52 A F♯m D V 3 Em
I grew u-p a child that no one want-ed. Not
57 A D
know-ing the ess-ence of love a child should fee-l. I grew cold - yet
61 G Em A
wish-ed for love and plead-ed. Then Anne found me and for a-while love was
65 D V 2 Em
real. I'm damn lone-ly this De-cem-ber morn-ing. Her

69
3
A D
name was Anne and our love was once bit - ter sweet. I re - call - her
73
G Em A
words u - pon my leav-ing. 'I hope you find a love that you can
77
D G D A D
Chorus
share.' Love is con - fu-sion and il - lu-sions. My lone - ly heart has no home. On a
82
Em A F♯m D
cold De-cem - ber morn-ing these emp - ty streets I roam. On a
86
End
Em A F♯m D
cold De-cem - ber morn-ing these emp - ty streets I roam.
90
Em A F♯m D

Free From Your Chain

Lyrics by
Richard Mousseau

Score by
Richard Mousseau

♩=76 Country Blues
Intro
C C6 Caug C G Em C C6 Caug C
V 1
No one can tell how I
G D G Am D G
feel in - side. I don't smile, I don't frown. I've got my pride. You can say what you
C G Am D G Em C C6 Caug
V 2
will. You can lie to your friends when asked, just pre - tend to cry. I won't re -
C G D G Am D G
veal all the hurt I feel, of the pieces of my heart you did steal. And yet still, yes I'll
C G Am D G Em
take all the shame and let your friends all think that I am to blame.
C G Em Am D G
Chorus
But the hurt it will end when I'm free from your chain, free to find true
Am Em C C6 Caug C G D G
Bridge
lo-ve to soothe my pain.

684 Walls Rd. Prince Twp., Ontario Canada P6A 6K4
mooseenterprises@on.aibn.com www.moosehidebooks.com

47 Am D G C G Am D 2
54 G Em C C6 Caug C G D G
V 3
One day the truth it will haunt your thoughts, and the truth that you
61 Am D G C G Am
hide will be caught. But yet now all your lies they still hurt. And the friends I once
67 D G Em C G Em
Chorus
had they treat me like dirt. But the hurt it will end when I'm
73 Am D G Am
free from your chain, free to find true lo - ve to soothe my
77 Em G Am Em C
End
pain. True lo - ve to soothe my pain.

Give Your Heart A Chance

Lyrics by
Richard Mousseau

Score by
Richard Mousseau

♩=82 Classic Country Blues
Intro
F C G7 C
V 1
When the long
night is still, you feel a deep wint-er's chill. There is a haunt-ing lone - ly-ness when
your heart will con - fess.
V 2
That true - love it has fail-ed. Your one and on-ly has
bail-ed. And through the long lone-ly nights you cry. You ask your - self why? He
Chorus
teas-ed your ten - der heart be - fore he cheat-ed with glee. He play-ed you for a
fool - . Yes ev - ery one can see. Your love for him was blind. Yes
right - from the start. But now please find some-one new to mend your brok - en

684 Walls Rd. Prince Twp., Ontario Canada P6A 6K4
mooseenterprises@on.aibn.com www.moosehidebooks.com

36
C F G7 C
Bridge
2
heart.
41
F G7 C
V 3
When the wint-er
46
F G7 C
winds turn warm you will have weather-ed the storm. With spring there will come a
50
F G7 C G7
Chorus
new ro-mance, just give your heart a chance. He teas-ed your ten - der heart be -
55
F C G7 F
fore he cheat-ed with glee. He play-ed you for a fool - . Yes ev - ery one can
60
C G7 F C
see. Your love for him was blind. Yes right - from the start. But
65
F C G7 C
now please find some - one new to mend your brok - en heart.
69
V 3
F G7 C
When the wint-er winds turn warm you will have weather-ed the storm. With

73
F
G7
3
spring there will come a new ro-mance, just give your heart a
76
C
F
G7
C
chance.

I Bid A Farewell

Lyrics by
Richard Mousseau

Score by
Richard Mousseau

♩=112 Celtic
Intro
Dm F Dm F
V 1
Will you wait each night on the
G Gm C F Dm
mull as the mist rolls in from the sea. Please wait for my ship to re -
F Dm F G Gm
turn home to Dun - dee. I have sailed at tide a first mate, as her tears ap -
C F Dm F Dm
peared u-pon her cheek. I bid her fare-well for ad - ven - ture I shall seek. Lone-ly
F G Am
Chorus
is a sail-or's life. Far from home u-pon the wind a ship of sails will won-der and
D G Gm C F
roam. A sail-or's chant will tell a tale of a love - r's heart bound to sail on a sea of
C F Dm F Dm F
Bridge
dreams home-ward bound.

684 Walls Rd. Prince Twp., Ontario Canada P6A 6K4
mooseenterprises@on.aibn.com www.moosehidebooks.com

36 G Gm C F Dm F 2
42 Dm F G Gm C F
48 Dm F Dm F
Chorus
Lone-ly is a sail-or's life. Far from
53 G Am D G
home u-pon the wind a ship of sails will won-der and roam. A sail-or's chant will tell a
58 Gm C F C F
tale of a love-r's heart bound to sail on a sea of dreams home-ward bound.
63 Dm F Dm F G Gm
V1
Men have sailed at tide at first wind with the tears of
68 C F Dm F Dm
loves left be - hind. They bid a fare-well and they pray the winds to be kind. My love
73 F G Gm C
waits no more on the mull for the years have passed one and

77
F Dm F Dm
3
three. I bid a fare-well, now to sleep be-neath the sea.

I Made A Mistake

Lyrics by
Richard Mousseasu

Score by
Richard Mousseau

♩=104 Pop / Rock
Intro
G♭m G♯m E
V 1
I thought I loved you, but I made a mis-
6
A G♯m E G♭m
take. In your self-ish ways all you do is take, and take.
11
G♯m E A
V 2
I thought I loved you, but you lied from the start. I gave you
15
G♯m E G♭m
Chorus
all my love, then you broke my heart, my heart will nev-er trust love a-
20
G♯m A E G♭m
gain. From a wo-man who mines for gold to satis-fy a self-ish gain, a pro-
25
A E G♭m G♯m
Bridge
fess-ion as old as time.
30
A E G♭m A E G♭m

2
V 2
I thought I loved you, but you lied from the start. I gave you
all my love, then you broke my heart, my heart
Chorus
will nev-er trust love a - gain. From a wo-man who mines for gold to satis-fy a self-ish gain, a pro-
fess-ion as old as time.
V 3
I thought I loved you, but
your heart was so cold. I gave you my true love but all my worth you stole, you
stole.
V 2
I thought I loved you, but you lied from the
start. I gave you all my love, then you broke my heart, my heart will
Chorus
nev-er trust love a - gain. From a wo-man who mines for gold to

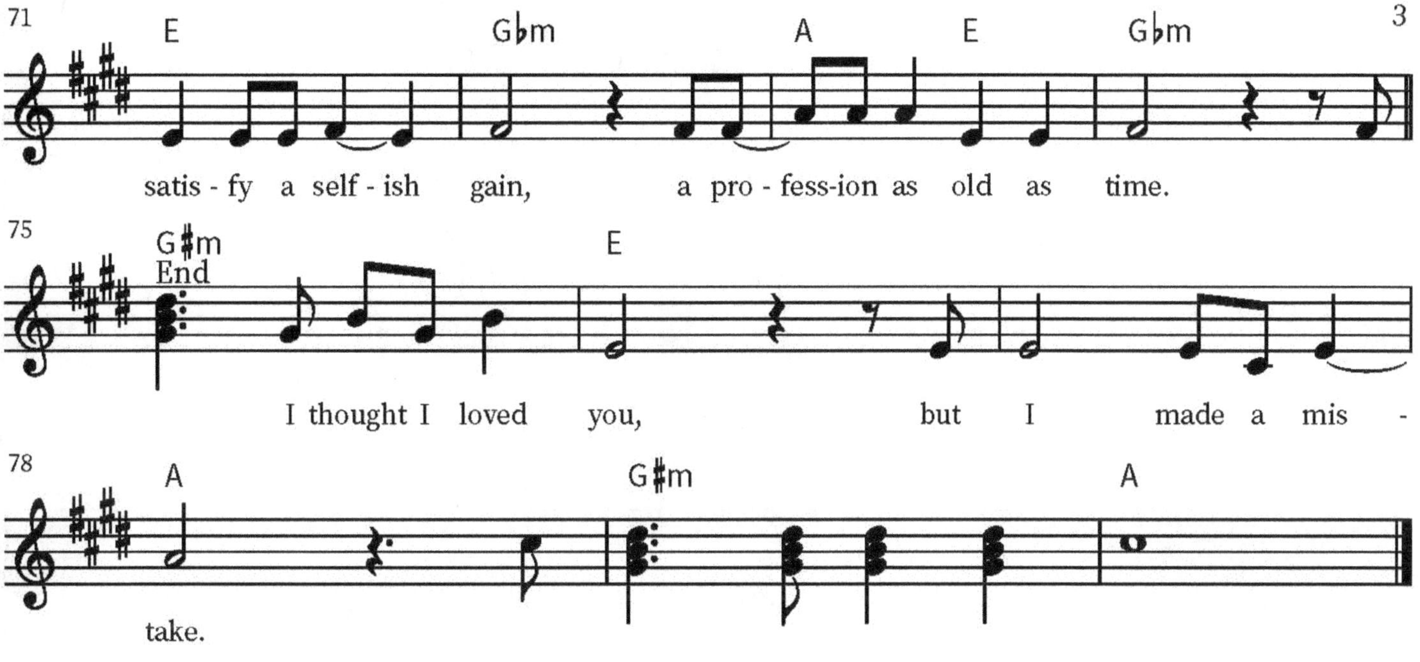
71
E
G♭m
A
E
G♭m
3
satis - fy a self - ish gain, a pro - fess-ion as old as time.
75
G♯m
End
E
I thought I loved you, but I made a mis -
78
A
G♯m
A
take.

I Really Want To Know

Lyrics by
Richard Mousseau

Score by
Richard Mousseau

♩=88 Classic Country
Intro
F D G C C6 Caug
6
V.1
C F C D G
You've told me it's ov - er, and he's not on your mind. Yet there's a pic-ture of
11
C C7 F Fm
him that I did find. By chance, in your dreams, do you call out his
16
C C6 Caug C F D G
name, your first love the first man who spark-ed love's first flame?
21
C C6 Caug C F C D
V.2
He held you so ten - der, the way I try to do. yet
26
G C C7 F
there's a mo-ment when I think you're blue. And thoughts come to mind of his
31
Fm C C6 Caug C F D
arms out to claim his first love, the first time you spark-ed love's first

684 Walls Rd. Prince Twp., Ontario Canada P6A 6K4
mooseenterprises@on.aibn.com www.moosehidebooks.com

36
G C C6 C
Chorus
F G C
flame. Must I try to guess? Please Dar - ling con - fess? Do
42
C7 F D G C
V.3
you still love him so? Yes, I real-ly want to know? Please tell me how
47
F C D G
you feel, if I should stay or go? If there is doublt in your mind, I should
52
C C7 F Fm C C6 Caug
know? If he's your true love, then I should not blame,
57
C F D G C C6 C
your first love, the first man, who spark-ed love's first flame. Must
62
Chorus
F G C
I try to guess? Please Dar - ling con - fess? Do
66
C7 F D G
you still love him so? Yes, I real - ly want to know?

I Will Never Love Again

Lyrics by
Richard Mousseau

Score by
Richard Mousseau

684 Walls Rd. Prince Twp., Ontario Canada P6A 6K4
mooseenterprises@on.aibn.com www.moosehidebooks.com

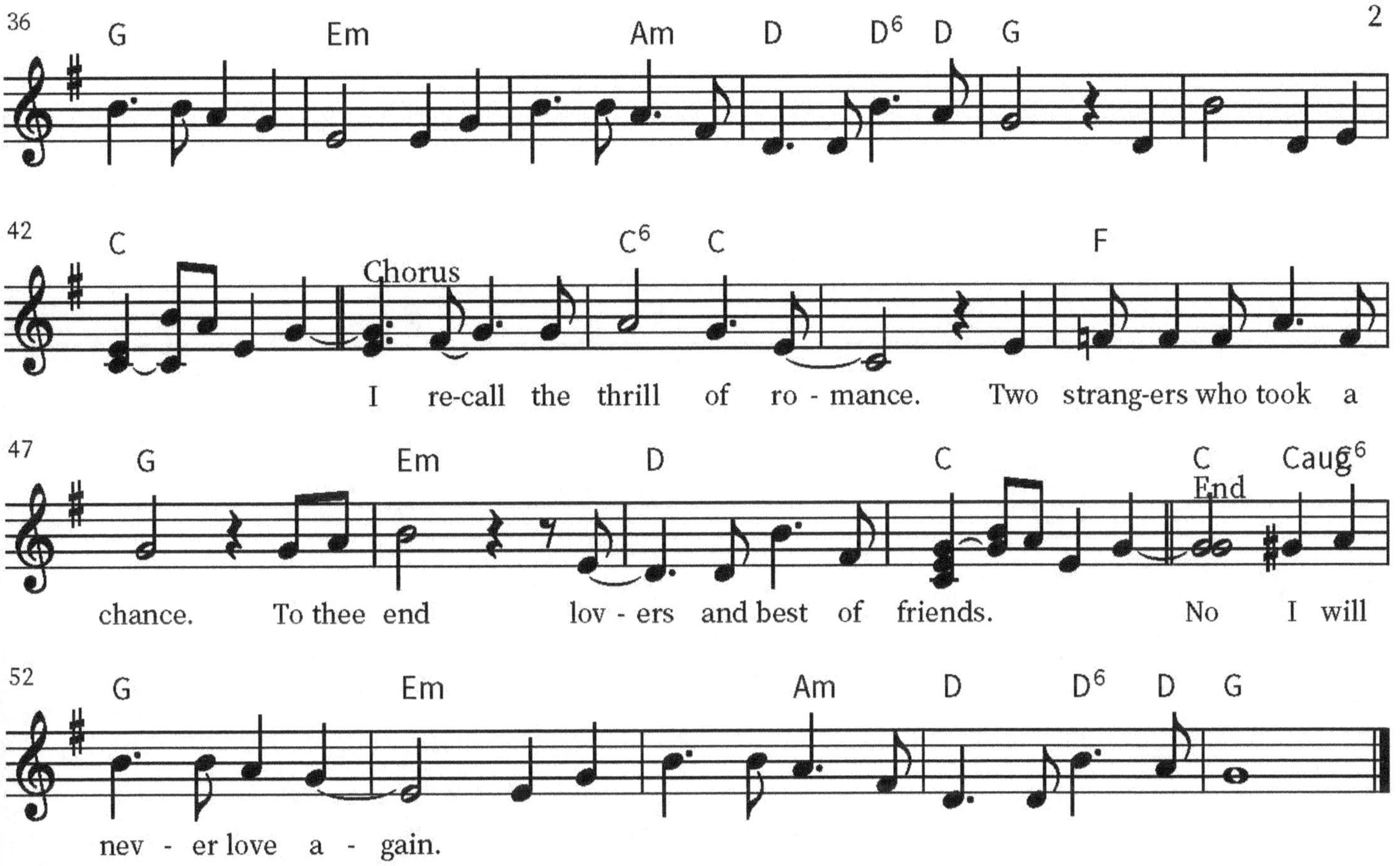
36
G Em Am D D6 D G
2
42
C C6 C F
Chorus
I re-call the thrill of ro - mance. Two strang-ers who took a
47
G Em D C C Caug6
End
chance. To thee end lov - ers and best of friends. No I will
52
G Em Am D D6 D G
nev - er love a - gain.

I Won't Walk away

Lyrics by
Richard Mousseau

Score by
Richard Mousseau

♩=120 Pop Rock
Intro
You
V 1
said I am a fool to care a-bout you. And the facts a-bout love I have no
clue. But I won't walk a - way, please let me stay.
V 2
Your man he was a fool, he left you to cry, and I know a-bout love and that is why I
will not walk a - way, please let me stay.
Chorus
I'll dry your te-ars, and calm your fears. And by your side I will sta-y. No I won't walk a - way.
Bridge
G C C7 F C6 B♭

684 Walls Rd. Prince Twp., Ontario Canada P6A 6K4
mooseenterprises@on.aibn.com www.moosehidebooks.com

38 C C7 C C7 F 2
I'll
44 C6 C F
Chorus
dry your te-ars, and calm your fears. And by your side I will
49 C6 C B♭ C G
V 3
sta-y. No I won't walk a - way. If he comes a - round then you just
54 C G C C7
say, I'm your man that you love and I will stay. No I won't walk a -
59 C C7 F G
V 1
way, for - ever I will stay. You said I am a fool to care a-bout
64 C G C C7
you. And the facts a-bout love I have no clue. But I won't walk a -
69 C C7 F C6 C
Chorus
way, please let me stay. I'll dry your te-ars, and calm your
75 F C6 C B♭ C
fears. And by your side I will sta-y. No I won't walk a - way. I'll

80
F
Chorus
C6 C
F
3
dry your te - ars, and calm your fears. And
84
C6 C
B♭
C
C6
by your side I will sta - y. No I won't walk a - way.

If You've Got The Time

Lyrics by
Richard Mousseau

Score by
Richard Mousseau

♩=108 Folk Rock
Intro
D D7 Bm G
V 1
I'm glad to see you it's
C Am D
been a - ges since I've been home. You were just a kid next door when
D7 G C
I be-gan to roam. Is my old house still stand - ing and does the door-bell still
Am D D7 Bm G
chime? Please tell me home-town tales if you've got the time?
Chorus
C D G
If you've got the time please tell me if Jen-ny speaks my name? And the
Am D G C
rea-son I left did she think she was to blame? If you've got the time please

684 Walls Rd. Prince Twp., Ontario Canada P6A 6K4
mooseenterprises@on.aibn.com www.moosehidebooks.com

32
D D7 Bm G
V 2
tell me if you've got the time? To say that I've been miss-
37
C Am D
ed by the girl I left be - hind. Does she wear my high-school pin, and
42
D7 G
does my name come to mind? If I ask will you tell me true? are my
46
C Am D D7 Bm
feel-ings for her too sub - lime? Please tell her I came by if you've got the
51
G C D G
Chorus
time? If you've got the time please tell me if Jen-ny speaks my
56
Am D G
name? And the rea-son I left please tell her I was to blame?
60
C D D7 Bm
If you've got the time please tell her if you've got the
65
G C D G
Bridge
time?

71
Am D G C D
3
77
D7 Bm G
V 3
C
Please tell my sweet Jen - ny I wish that I could
83
Am D D7 G
stay. If I could it would be nice to ling-er one more day. They
88
C Am D
say you can't change the past, but a first love will al-ways last. Please tell her I came
93
D7 Bm G
Chorus
C
by if you've got the time. If you've got the time please
98
D G Am D
tell me if Jen-ny speaks my name? And the rea-son I left please tell her I was to
103
G C
blame? If you've got the time please
106
D D7 Bm G
tell her if you've got the time?

I've Done Shopped Around

Lyrics by
Richard Mousseau

Score by
Richard Mousseau

684 Walls Rd. Prince Twp., Ontario Canada P6A 6K4
mooseenterprises@on.aibn.com www.moosehidebooks.com

36 C C7 G D G C C7 2
asked her to be mine, but she turn-ed me down, yes she turn-ed me
41 D G G7 G C
V 2
down. There's plent-y of fish in the sea so hook a good one. If you land a big old
46 C7 C A A7
shark just toss her back son. You got to find a ma-ma bear now, a sweet tur-tle -
50 A D D7 D G G7
Bridge
dove, A gal that will hang a - round and give you true love.
55 G C C7 C G G7 G
60 C C7 G D G C C7 D
I
66 G G7 G C
V 3
shop-ped in the church down town and in the bars I saw, plent-y of gals to a -
70 C7 C A A7
dore, so I told my old Pa. He said no mat-ter what you do it's a gam-ble my

son. There's plent-y of gals a - round that want to have fun.
Chorus
I've done shop-ped a - round, and look what I've found, a gal so sweet and
fine. I asked her to be mine, and she did-n't turn me down, no
End
Bridge
she did-n't turn me down. She did-n't turn me down,

I've Lost You Again

Lyrics by
Richard Mousseau

Score by
Richard Mousseau

♩=104 Country
Intro
Gm C C7 C6 C F Dm
V 1
I've been fool-ing my - self that you will stay. I've tried my best but your heart will
F
stray. It's just a matt-ter of when will I lose you a - gain.
B♭ C C7 C6 C F Dm
You know that I for - give the wrongs you've made I've felt your love each day slow-ly
F
fade. It's just a matt-ter of when will I lose you a - gain. It's
B♭ C C7 C6 C F
Chorus 1
Gm C F A
happen-ed be - fore, you've walked out our door. You came crawl-ing back, I
B♭ F Gm C C7 C6 C
helped you un - pack. This is now and that was then. Now I've lost you a -

684 Walls Rd. Prince Twp., Ontario Canada P6A 6K4
mooseenterprises@on.aibn.com www.moosehidebooks.com

2
35 F Dm Bridge F
gain.
41 B♭ C C7 C6 C F
It's
46 Gm Chorus 1 C F A
happen-ed be-fore, you've walked out our door. You came crawl-ing back, I
50 B♭ F Gm C C7 C6 C
helped you un-pack. This is now and that was then. Now I've lost you a-
55 F Dm V 2 F
gain. I've been wast-ing my life, but you don't care. I've tried my best to
60 B♭ C C7 C6 C
love, but you don't share. It's just a matt-ter of when will I lose you a-
65 F Dm F
gain. I've been fool-ing my-self that you will stay. I've tried my best but
70 B♭ C C7 C6 C
your heart will stray. It's just a matt-ter of when will I lose you a-

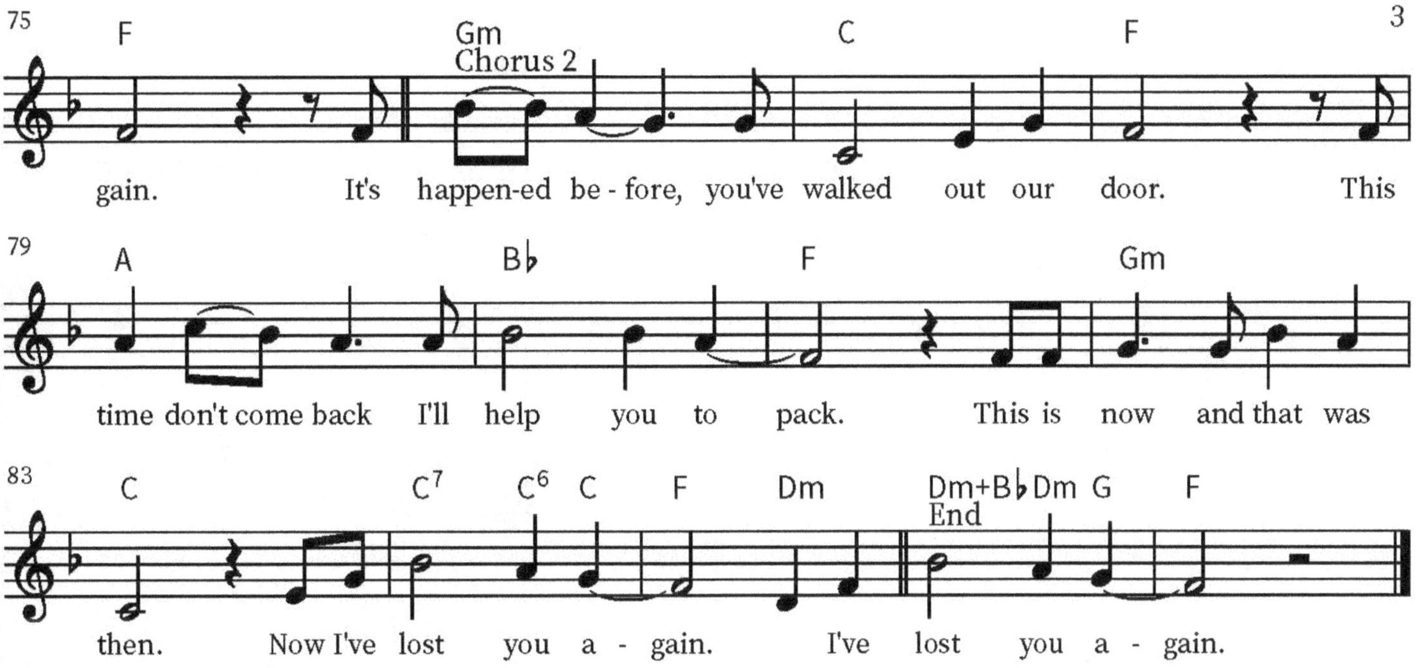
75
3
F Gm C F
Chorus 2
gain. It's happen-ed be - fore, you've walked out our door. This
79
A B♭ F Gm
time don't come back I'll help you to pack. This is now and that was
83
C C7 C6 C F Dm Dm+B♭Dm G F
End
then. Now I've lost you a - gain. I've lost you a - gain.

Just An Average Guy

Lyrics by
Richard Mousseau

Score by
Richard Mousseau

♩=108 Pop Classic 60's
Intro
G Am D
I'm
Chorus
G Am D
not the type of man - who treats a wo - man - - with dis-re - spect.
G Em Am D
Love from a man a wo - man should ex - pect from you. I've
G Am D
no-ticed at times that young girls will be sway-ed - - and fall for bad boys.
G Em Am D Em
V 1
It is a shame those men treat girls like toys it's true. Why do wo-men fall for the
G Am G Am
guy who acts so cool? When the ro-mance dies she'll know he played her for a
D Em G Am G
fool. She'll love the ride un-til the high be-gins to fall. He'll use her and leave her a

684 Walls Rd. Prince Twp., Ontario Canada P6A 6K4
mooseenterprises@on.aibn.com www.moosehidebooks.com

2
con-quest et-ched on the wall.
V 2
I'm a gen-tle man who will stand by and not turn tail. Just an aver-age guy, the
kind of man who will not fail. If wo-men would look be - yond a cad's pick-up
line, to find real men wait-ing to make her love life just fine.
Bridge
Chorus
I'm not the type of man - who treats a wo - man - with dis-re - spect.

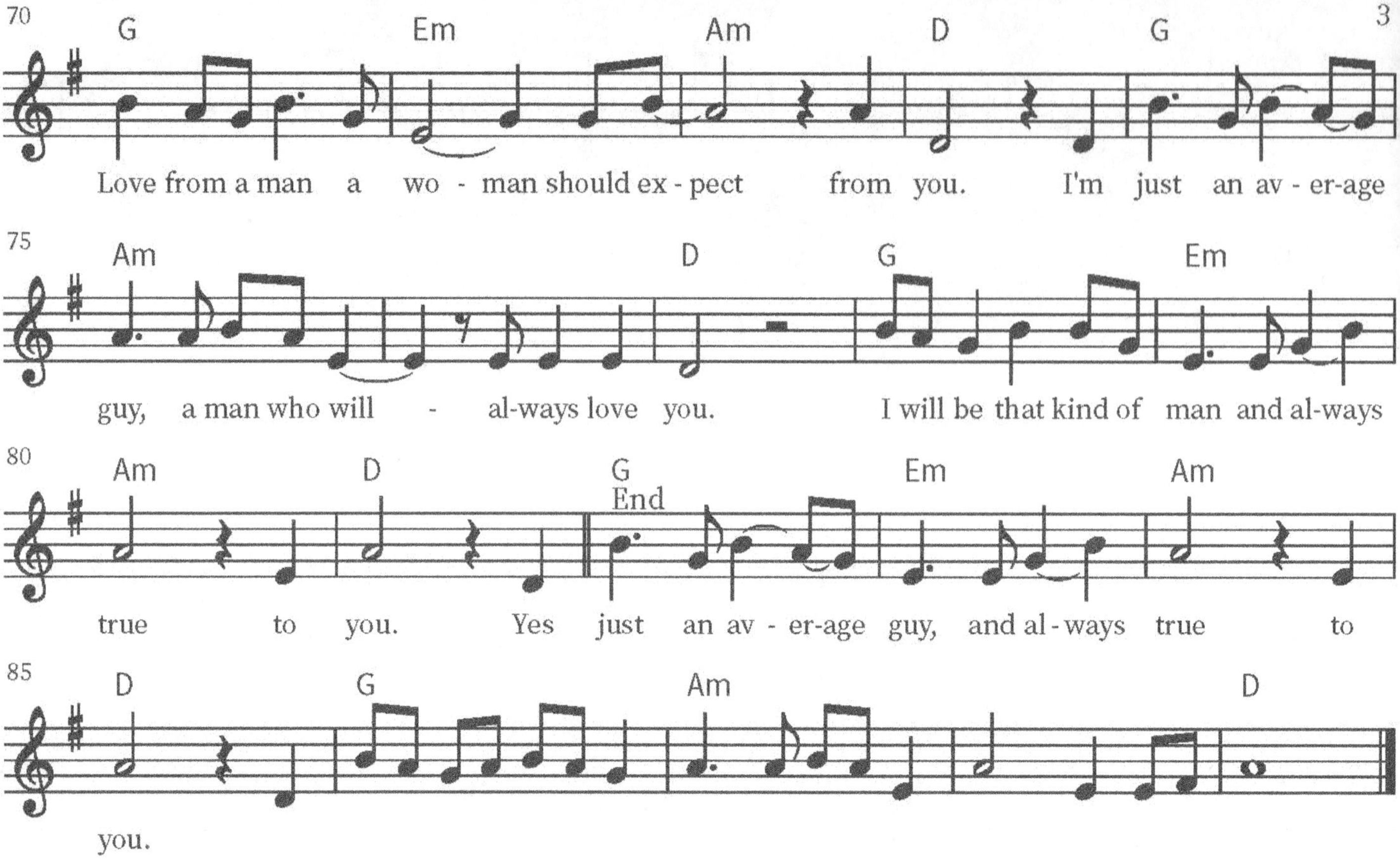
70
G Em Am D G
3
Love from a man a wo - man should ex - pect from you. I'm just an av - er-age
75
Am D G Em
guy, a man who will - al-ways love you. I will be that kind of man and al-ways
80
Am D G Em Am
End
true to you. Yes just an av - er-age guy, and al - ways true to
85
D G Am D
you.

Little Sister Loves To Boogie

Lyrics by
Richard Mousseau

Score by
Richard Mousseau

♩=130 Rockabilly
Intro
F A7 Gm A7 Dm
F Dm F
V 1
From the day she was born Pa said it was in her
Gm C7
feet. For nine months the house would jump with a boo - gie beat. Pa
A7 Dm
play-ed the bass and Ma sang Hill - bill - y rock. The joint was al-ways jump-ing I'm
A7 Dm F
Chorus
told a-round the clock. Yes lit- tle sis-ter loves to boo-gie - woo-gie, and jive and
A7 Gm A7 Dm
sway. She's a lit - tle jit - ter - bug. Yes she can shag dance and cut a rug. Yes
F Dm F
V 2
lit - tle sis - ter loves to boo - gie - woo-gie. From the day she was born her

684 Walls Rd. Prince Twp., Ontario Canada P6A 6K4
mooseenterprises@on.aibn.com www.moosehidebooks.com

29
Gm
C7
2
hips would shim-my and shake. Each night when the mu-sic would play the floors would
33
A7
Dm
quake. Her crib would be rock-ing and ba-by would be danc-ing a - way. My
37
A7
Dm
F
Chorus
sis-ter would nev - er cry, my Pa would say. Yes lit-tle sis-ter loves to boo-gie -
41
A7
Gm
woo-gie, and hop and swing. She's a lit-tle jit-ter - bug. Yes she can shag dance and
45
A7
Dm
F
Dm
F
Bridge
cut a rug. Yes lit-tle sis-ter loves to boo-gie - woo-gie.
49
Gm
C7
54
A7
Dm
A7
59
Dm
F

3
64 A7 Gm A7 Dm F Dm
From the
68 F V 3 Gm
day she was born Pa said lit-tle sis-ter has a chance. And through the years be a
72 C7 A7
star of the boo - gie dance. Each night the house still jumps with a boo - gie
76 Dm A7 Dm
beat. To watch lit - tle sis - ter cut a rug is a treat. Yes
80 F Chorus
lit-tle sis-ter loves to boo-gie - woo-gie, and jive and sway. She's a lit-tle jit-ter - bug. Yes she can
84 A7 Gm A7 Dm F Dm
shag dance and cut a rug. Yes lit - tle sis - ter loves to boo-gie - woo-gie. Yes
88 F Chorus
lit-tle sis-ter loves to boo-gie - woo-gie, and hop and swing. She's a lit-tle jit-ter - bug. Yes she can
92 A7 Gm A7 Dm F Dm
shag dance and cut a rug. Yes lit - tle sis - ter loves to boo-gie - woo-gie.

96
F
End
A7
Gm
4
99
A7
Dm
F
Dm

Love's Game In Cocamo

Lyrics by
Richard Mousseau

Score by
Richard Mousseau

♩=104 60's Pop
Intro
G
Chorus 1
Em
Do you ev - er think of me on the beach of Co-ca - mo, where the sand is warm, the girls all
Am D D6 D G Em
know how to play all night be-neath par-ty lights of Co - ca - mo.
G
Chorus 2
Em
Do you ev - er think of me when you dance in Co-ca - mo, where the men all tease the girls, I
Am D D6 D G Em
know how we play the game be-neath the stars of Co - ca - mo.
Am
V1
D
I was that type of guy who would dance and charm a girl with ro -
G Em
mance un-til sil-ver wings would fly her a - way. But I fell in love deep-er each day. Yet

684 Walls Rd. Prince Twp., Ontario Canada P6A 6K4
mooseenterprises@on.aibn.com www.moosehidebooks.com

Am D D6 D G Em
2
you were here I know to play love's game in Co - ca - mo.
G Em Am
Bridge
D D6 D G Em Am
D G Em
Am D D6 D
G Em G
Chorus 2
Do you ev - er think of me when you dance in Co - ca -
Em Am
mo, where the men all tease the girls, I know how we play the game be-neath the
D D6 D G Em Am
V1
stars of Co - ca - mo. I was that type of guy who would

68
D
G
3
dance and charm a girl with ro - mance un - til sil - ver wings would fly her a -
72
Em
Am
way. But I fell in love deep-er each day. Yet you were here I know to play love's
77
D D6 D G
Em
D D6 D G
End
game in Co - ca - mo.

MoJo

Lyrics by
Richard Mousseau

Score by
Richard Mousseau

♩= 108 Rock Blues
Intro
G
V 1
Mo-Jo he comes from no-where then sit's him-self
down. Mo-Jo he picks an old flat-top as peo-ple gath-er round. His
C C7 D
voice tells a tale of a life of soul-ful blues. Ev-ery song he sings brings
G
V 2
vis-sions of tra-gic news. Mo-Jo can't see his days are dark as the night.
C
Mo-Jo met the De-vil as a child and the De-vil took the light. He now tells the truth to
C7 D G
those who do not know. As the flat-top moans and cries a haunt-ing ec-ho. The
C C7 C6 C D D6 D
Chorus
blues were born in his tor-ment-ed soul. He's liv-ing a life, that's filled with strife. No

684 Walls Rd. Prince Twp., Ontario Canada P6A 6K4
mooseenterprises@on.aibn.com www.moosehidebooks.com

32 G G7 Em D Nc G C C7 2
Bridge
gos - pel song can heal his tor-tured soul.
37 C6 C D D6 D G G7 Em
42 D Nc G
V.3
Mo-Jo met a de-mon one morn - ing in the del-ta
46
mist. The de-vil offer-ed gold and fame no child could re - sist. Though
50 C C7 D
temp-ted a blind-man could see through a li - er's tale. Mo-jo told the De-vil his
54 G
V.4
soul was not for sale. To play and sing the blues was all he did crave.
59 C
Mo-Jo made a deal and his soul the child would save. I will make you great said the
63 C7 D
De-vil, a sing-er of the blues. In ex - change I'll take your sight, this you will

3
Chorus
lose. The blues were born in his tor-ment-ed soul. He's liv-ing a life, that's
filled with strife. No gos - pel song can heal his tor - tured soul.
V 5
Mo-Jo he comes from no-where then sit's him-self down.
Mo-Jo he picks an old flat-top as peo-ple gath-er round. His song tells a tale of a
deal the De-vil had made. And tells of a price that Mo-Jo once had paid. The
Chorus
blues were born in his tor-ment-ed soul. He's liv-ing a life, that's filled with strife. No
gos - pel song can heal his tor - tured soul.
End

My Gal In Moosonee

Lyrics by
Richard Mousseau

Score by
Richard Mousseau

♩=132 Country rock
Intro
E
V 1
I have a sweet gal up in Moose - o-nee, and bless her heart she is
A
B7
wait-ing for me. When I left I know I did her wrong. I nev-er ment to be
E
gone so long. The prom-ise I made was a down-right lie. The guilt I had, I
A
B7
won't de - ny. I said I'd be gone oh not too long. But deep in-side I know I
E
Chorus
A
B7
did her wrong. I want to go home, nev - er more to roam. I long to
E
E
Bridge
see my gal in Moose-o - nee

684 Walls Rd. Prince Twp., Ontario Canada P6A 6K4
mooseenterprises@on.aibn.com www.moosehidebooks.com

2
A
B7 E
A B7 E
The
E
V 2
stor-ies I've heard they teased my mind, but big city life was not so kind. I
A B7 E
told my gal that I was fine. I did not say for her I pine. The hec-tic city life is
A
not for me. I long to be in Moose-o - nee where I can breath the north-ern air, and
B7 E A
Chorus
be with my gal our lives to share. I want to go home, nev - er more to roam. I
B7 E
long to see my gal in Moose-o - nee I

V 1
have a sweet gal up in Moose - o-nee, and bless her heart she is wait-ing for me.
When I left I know I did her wrong. I nev-er ment to be gone so long.
Bridge
Chorus
I want to go home, nev - er more to roam. I long to see my gal in Moose-o - nee
Chorus
I want to go home, nev - er more to roam. I long to see my gal in Moose - o - nee

Not My First Rodeo

Lyrics by
Richard Mousseau

Score by
Richard Mousseau

♩=108 Clasic Country
Intro
Chorus
Ba-by I know
that you don't care if I stay or go. I've hung a-round too long for you to
bear. This is not my first ro - de - o.
V 1
It's plain - to see you're
ti-red of me. I can't de-ny, I won't lie, I did my best, but now I'm a pest. You
want some-one new so I'll say a-dieu.
V 2
I hog - the bed so you said. I'm
too damn sweet and burp when I eat. I cud-dle all wrong. It's the same old song. That
men are to blame for love's dy-ing flame.
Bridge
G C D D6 Am Em

2
34 C G D
39 D6 D G C Am
45 G Em D6 D G G
Chorus
Ba-by I know
50 C
that you don't care if I stay or go. I've hung a-round too long for you to
55 G D D6 D G C
V 3
bear. This is not my first ro - de - o. It's plain - to see it's not
60 Am G
meant to be. I can't de-ny I won't lie. You're to blame for love's dy-ing flame. You
65 Em D6 D G G
Chorus
made me blue, so I'll say a-dieu. Ba-by I know that you don't care if I
70 C G D
stay or go. I've hung a-round too long for you to bear. This is not my first
75 D6 D G G
End
ro - de - o. Ba-by you know,

81
C
G
D
3
this is not my first
85
D6
D
G
3
Nc
G
ro - de - o.

On Monday I'm Blue

Lyrics by
Richard Mousseau

Score by
Richard Mousseau

♩=104 Pop Rock
Intro
C Caug F7 G Gaug G
On
V 1
C F7 G Gaug G C
Mon-day I'm feel-ing blue, be - cause I'm poor it's true. On Tues-day I ask my-self
G Gaug G C
why I work so hard to try, on Wends-day to pay her bills, and
F7 G Gaug G C
work a doub-ble at the mill. Come Thurs-day I'm beat to the bone. My
Chorus
G C F G
life the bank does own. On Fri-day my gal takes my pay then spends it all Sa-tur-
C F G C
day. On Sun-day on my knees to pray, to the poor-house I'm on my way. Yes it's
V 2
C F7 G Gaug G C
true I love my gal, but a dog is a cheap-er pal. But when I get home at

684 Walls Rd. Prince Twp., Ontario Canada P6A 6K4
mooseenterprises@on.aibn.com www.moosehidebooks.com

35
G Gaug G C
night, her lov-ing is sweet de - light. Yes it's true I've paid the price, and
40
F7 G Gaug G C G
if you want my ad - vice, go out and find a hon - ey that has her own damn
45
C F G C
Chorus
mon-ey.
50
F G C C
V 1
On Mon-day I'm feel-ing
55
F7 G Gaug G C
blue, be - cause I'm poor it's true. On Tues-day I ask my-self why I
60
G Gaug G C
work so hard to try, on Wends-day to pay her bills, and
64
F7 G Gaug G C
work a doub-ble at the mill. Come Thurs-day I'm beat to the bone. My
68
G C F G
Chorus
life the bank does own. On Fri-day my gal takes my pay then spends it all Sa-tur-

73
C F G C
3
day. On Sun-day on my knees to pray, to the poor-house I'm on my way. On
78
C G
Mon-day I'm feel - ing blue, be - cause I'm poor it's
81
C Nc Gaug G Gaug C
End
true.

Our Home

Lyrics by
Richard Mousseau

Score by
Richard Mousseau

684 Walls Rd. Prince Twp., Ontario Canada P6A 6K4
mooseenterprises@on.aibn.com www.moosehidebooks.com

37 G7 Am C 2
Bridge
A house left emp-ty is not a home an - y more.
42 F C G7
I long for the laugh - ter and joy we once
48 C F C G7
had. But now our
54 Am C C7 F
Chorus
lives seem so cold and so sad. We raised some kids we
59 C G7 C D7
loved and a pet or two. And through the years of change our love stayed
64 G7 C Nc C F C
true. But there comes a time when life will close a door.
69 G7 Am C
V 1
A house left emp-ty is not a home an - y more. Our home at the
74 F C G7
end of the street sits emp - ty, long-ing for the laugh - ter and

79
C
F
C
3
joy it once had. Our neigh-bours at times would hide their en-vy.
85
G7
Am
C
End
But now our home seems so cold and so sad. I long for the
90
G7
C
Nc
laugh - ter and joy we once had.

Road of Regret

Lyrics by
Richard Mousseau

Score by
Richard Mousseau

♩=92 Country Folk Rock
Intro
F C A Dm
V 1
F C A Dm
What do you do with wast - ed dreams from the past that you re - call? Do you
B♭ Gm C Dm F
won-der if she thinks of you at all? In mis - ty view you
C A Dm B♭ Gm
try to see a face from the past. When the ro-mance that you had, you thought would
C Dm
last.
Chorus
Gm B♭ C
Your shat-tered dreams and wast - ed schemes you try to for -
Dm A G C F Dm
get. Yet leave a trail of tears and fears on a road of re - gret.
V 2
F C A Dm
What do you do when you find out the girl from your past is with a friend? And the

684 Walls Rd. Prince Twp., Ontario Canada P6A 6K4
mooseenterprises@on.aibn.com www.moosehidebooks.com

34 B♭ Gm C Dm F 2
love for you was a game of pre - tend? In mis - ty view you
39 C A Dm B♭ Gm
try to see just where you went wrong. But the love you gave to her was not that
44 C Dm Gm B♭ C
Chorus
strong. Your shat-tered dreams and wast - ed schemes you try to for -
49 Dm A G C F Dm
get. Yet leave a trail of tears and fears on a road of re - gret.
54 F C A Dm
V 3
What do you do with wast - ed dreams from the past that you re - call? Do you
58 B♭ Gm C Dm F
won-der if some-one thinks of you at all? You turn-ed your back on
63 C A Dm B♭ Gm
folks back home to live a lust-ful life. Now the cold-ness in your heart cuts like a
68 C Dm Gm B♭ C
Chorus
knife. Your shat-tered dreams and wast - ed schemes you try to for -

73
Dm A G C F Dm
3
get. Yet leave a trail of tears and fears on a road of re - gret.

Somewhere, Someone Waits

Lyrics by
Richard Mousseau

Score by
Richard Mousseau

♩=88 Pop
Intro
C6 C F C F C6 C
V 1
Some-where out
Am F C F B♭
there some-one waits for love to come their way. Some-one will break some-one's
Am F C G
heart, and lost love hap-pens each day. Love is just a game peop-le
D B♭ C C6 C Am
play in search of a con-quest to a - buse. Some-where out there love will
F C F C6 C Am F
V 2
last, though some are sure to lose. Some-times el - ders wish to have some-
C F B♭ Am F
one just to hold. Some-one to say just have fun, en-joy life, you're not too
C G D B♭
old. Is love a roll of dice? peop-le play in hope that they may win the -

40 C C6 C Am F C F 2
game. Some-where out there love is lost each day; who is to blame?
46 C6 C Am F C F
Bridge
V 3
Some-one will
52 B♭ Am F C
Bridge
break some-one's heart, and lost love hap-pens each day.
57 G D B♭ C C6 C Am
V 4
Some-where out there some-one
63 F C F
waits for love to come their way.
66 C6 C F C F
End

Sweet Ruby

Lyrics by
Richard Mousseau

Score by
Richard Mousseau

♩=122 60's Rock
Intro
A Bm D
There's a
6
V 1
G
sweet lit-tle girl I - know and her name is Ru - by. She lives down the road and she
10
A Bm
makes me want to smile. Walk-ing hand in hand with this gal mi-ght be fu -
14
G D G
tile. She is one of a kind that kid down the road nam-ed Ru - by. Sweet
18
A Bm D
Ru - by Ru - by I knew right from the start you owned my heart. There's a
22
V 2
G
chance ev-ery day I will walk to school with Ru - by. I won't ta - lk much but I
26
A Bm
know what I'd like to say. But the words in my head they sound like a cheap cli -

684 Walls Rd. Prince Twp., Ontario Canada P6A 6K4
mooseenterprises@on.aibn.com www.moosehidebooks.com

30
G D G A
2
che`. She thinks I'm cute but kind of weird says Ru - by. Sweet Ru - by Ru - by I
35
Bm D G
Chorus
knew right from the start you owned my heart. When she breaks oth - er boys'
39
G♯dim D Daug Bm A
hearts, it's my chance with ro - mance, be-cause Ru - by Ru - by I
43
Bm D A
Bridge
knew right from the start you owned my heart.
48
Bm D G G♯dimD Daug
53
Bm A Bm D
There's a
58
V.3
G
chance one day my life will be with Ru - by. When we tu-rn eight I'll ask her to be
63
A Bm G
mine. If she holds my hand and smiles I'll know it's a sign. She is

67
D G A
3
one of a kind that kid down the road nam-ed Ru - by. Sweet Ru - by Ru - by I
71
Bm D G
Chorus
knew right from the start you owned my heart. When she breaks oth-er boys'
75
G♯dim D Daug Bm A
hearts, it's my chance with ro - mance, be-cause Ru - by Ru - by I
79
Bm D Bm
knew right from the start you owned my heart. Sweet
82
A
End
Bm D
Ru - by Ru - by I knew right from the start you owned my heart.

Tell Me Why You Cry

Lyrics by
Richard Mousseau

Score by
Richard Mousseau

2
38 D E♭m C Cm C G G♭ Em Am D G
Bridge
a.
44 D E♭m C C6 C D Bm Em Bm
50 D E♭m C Cm C G G♭ Em Am D
Chorus
They tell me that you seek sym-path - y, a need to
55 G D E♭m C C6 C D Bm
have my loy - al - ty, so you lie to me, and you cry. You used my e - mo -
60 Em Bm D E♭m C Cm C Cm D
V 3
tions, a-bused my de - vo - tion. So tell me why, oh
65 G GmG Em G D E♭m C C6 C
why that I should stay, when I know yes I know the game you play - a - a -
70 D E♭m C Cm C Cm D G GmG Em
V 4
a. Tell me why, please tell me why you lie? Tell me
75 G D E♭m C C6 C D Bm
why you need to lie and why you cry? - i - i - i. why you cry?

Thee Essence Of You

Lyrics by
Richard Mousseau

Score by
Richard Mousseau

=92 Classic Country
Intro
F G C C6 G
These
6
V 1
troub-les of the day I can't re - solve. The puz-zel of this life I can't
11
C D G
solve. The truth be told, I will not lie. A - lone at night with -
16
Am C C6 G
V 2
out you I do cry. Each day I a - wake from dreams of you. The
21
C D
laugh-ter we had is gone. My day be-comes blue. The warmth that you
25
G Am C
gave is now so cold. And nev-er a - gain your hand will I hold. To em-
30
F Gm C F
Chorus
brace you once more and feel your sweet kiss. Thee ess - ence of you, the

684 Walls Rd. Prince Twp., Ontario Canada P6A 6K4
mooseenterprises@on.aibn.com www.moosehidebooks.com

34
G C F G C C62
touch of you I will miss. Thee em - brace of you, thee ess - ence of you I will
39
C F Gm C F
Bridge
miss.
44
G C F G C C6
49
G
V 2
Each day I a - wake from dreams of you. The laugh-ter we had is
54
C D G
gone. My day be-comes blue. The warmth that you gave is now so cold. And
59
Am C F Gm
Chorus
nev-er a-gain your hand will I hold. To em - brace you once more and feel your sweet
64
C F G C F
kiss. Thee ess-ence of you, the touch of you I will miss. Thee em - brace of you, thee
69
G C C6 G F
End
ess - ence of you I will miss. Thee ess - ence of you, the

73
G
C
3
touch of you I will miss.

Time Passes By

Lyrics by
Richard Mousseau

Score by
Richard Mousseau

♩=98 Rock
Intro
A Bm A A6 A C♯ A F♯m
V 1
I've liv-ed through the
7
A F♯m E F♯m
years of my youth in search of life's mean-ings, and truths.
12
A F♯m E Bm
Now I sit and watch time fly by, con-tem-plating my ques-tions of
17
C♯ F♯m C♯ F♯m E F♯m A
V 2
why-y has time passed on by. I've watch-ed my child-ren at play when so
22
F♯m E F♯m A
young. Then smiled when I re-call the songs they've sung. Now I sit and
27
F♯m E Bm C♯ F♯m C♯
watch time fly by. Mem-or-ies some-times will let me cry-y-y, as
32
F♯m E A Bm A C♯ A E
Chorus
time will pass me by. Ti-i-ime pass-es by in a blink of an

684 Walls Rd. Prince Twp., Ontario Canada P6A 6K4
mooseenterprises@on.aibn.com www.moosehidebooks.com

2
38
A C♯ A A6 A Bm A C♯ A E
eye - - e. Ti - i - ime pass-es by in a blink of an
44
A C♯ A A6 A Bm A A6 A C♯ A
eye - e - e. Ti - i - ime. Ti - i - ime.
50
Bridge
F♯m A F♯m E F♯m
56
A F♯m E Bm
61
C♯ F♯mC♯ F♯m E F♯m A
V 3
To be a-lone with age is a
66
F♯m E F♯m A
crime. The mind will watch the pass - ing of time. Here I sit a -
71
F♯m E Bm C♯ F♯mC♯
lone to watch life's fools. They don't stop to fol-low a sim - ple rul - e - e. Don't
76
F♯m E A Bm A C♯ A E
Chorus
let time pass on by. Ti - i - ime pass-es by in a blink of an

82
A C♯ A A6 A Bm A C♯ A E
3
eye - - e. Ti - i - ime pass-es by in a blink of an
88
A C♯ A A6 A Bm A A6 A C♯ A
eye - e - e. Ti - i - ime. Ti - i - ime.

Too Many Tears

Lyrics by
Richard Mousseau

Score by
Richard Mousseau

♩=96 60's Ballad
Intro
G Nc Em Nc G Nc Em D C
Am D C D G Em C D G Am
Chorus
You cried too man-y tears and wast - ed too many years a-lone be -
D G Em C D D+d♭ C
V 1
hind a wall in wait for your child to call. What do you do when your
Am Em D Am
child runs a-way? What could you have done to make them stay? Was love not e-nough? Were
Em C Am D D+d♭ C D
Chorus
you too strict? What did you do or say to cause such con-flict? You cried
G Em C D G Am D G Em C
too man-y tears and wast - ed too many years a-lone be - hind a wall in wait for your child to
D D+d♭ C Am
V 2
call. You give your child what you nev-er had. You

684 Walls Rd. Prince Twp., Ontario Canada P6A 6K4
mooseenterprises@on.aibn.com www.moosehidebooks.com

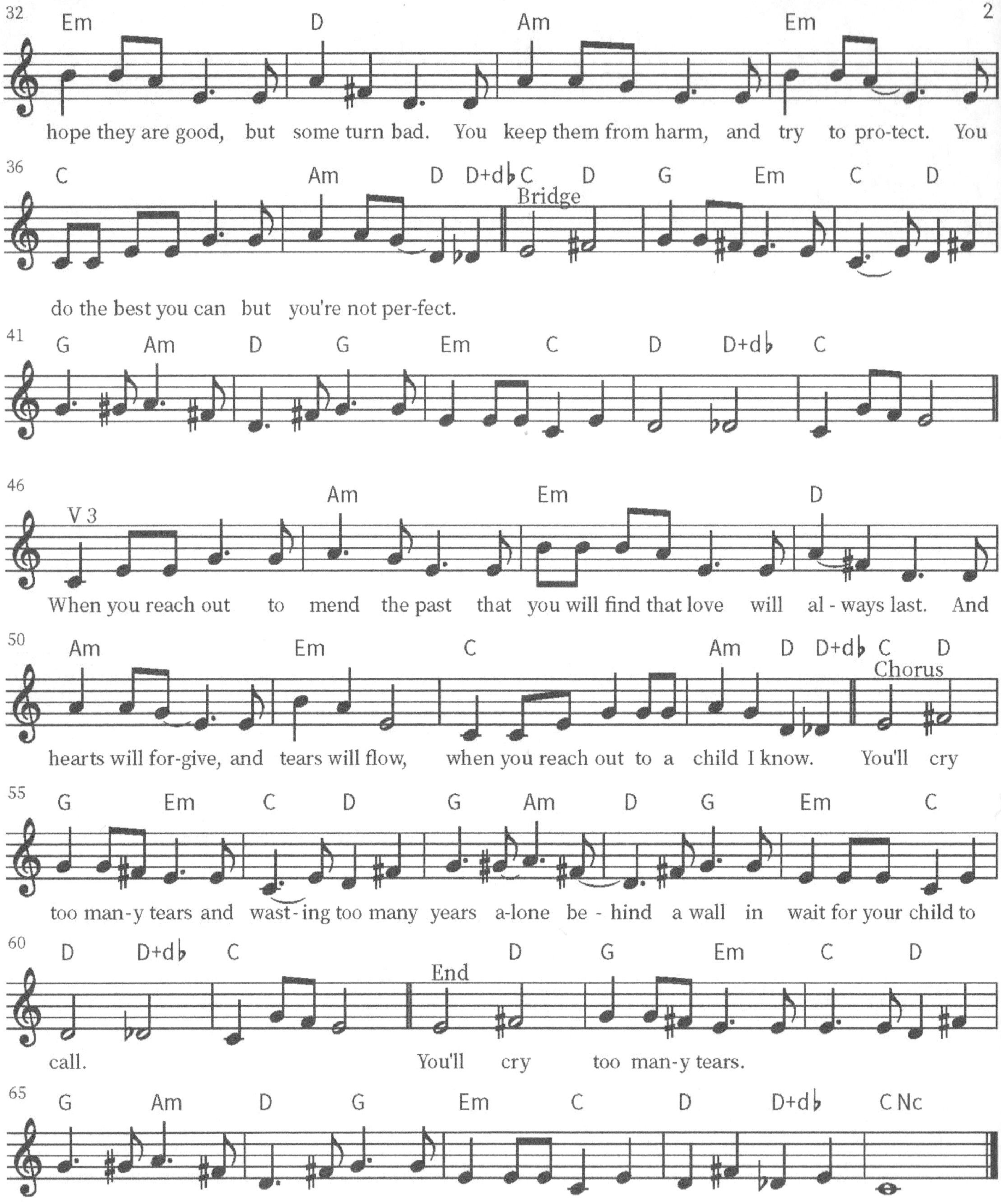
2
Em D Am Em
hope they are good, but some turn bad. You keep them from harm, and try to pro-tect. You
C Am D D+d♭ C D G Em C D
Bridge
do the best you can but you're not per-fect.
G Am D G Em C D D+d♭ C
V 3
Am Em D
When you reach out to mend the past that you will find that love will al - ways last. And
Am Em C Am D D+d♭ C D
Chorus
hearts will for-give, and tears will flow, when you reach out to a child I know. You'll cry
G Em C D G Am D G Em C
too man-y tears and wast-ing too many years a-lone be - hind a wall in wait for your child to
D D+d♭ C D G Em C D
End
call. You'll cry too man-y tears.
G Am D G Em C D D+d♭ C Nc

We Were Best Of Friends

Lyrics by
Richard Mousseau

Score by
Richard Mousseau

684 Walls Rd. Prince Twp., Ontario Canada P6A 6K4
mooseenterprises@on.aibn.com www.moosehidebooks.com

32
G C G
V 2
2
Then one day he came a - long, and stole my sweet gal from me. So I just
37
D C D G
left and pack-ed my bags, and wished them well, and now I'm free. like a
41
C G
fool I wand-ered far. But when that old moon is bright, I think of that
45
D C D G
Chorus
gal I left back home. They say for love I should fight. We were best of friends all
50
C Am D G
sum - mer long. And year af - ter year our love grew strong. Then came the sum-mer of
54
A D G D G
chance, some say a first ro-mance. We did in-tend to be best of friends.
59
D G C Am
Bridge
64
D G A D G

V.3
Here I sit with my sweet
gal, and live by the old grist mill. And tell our kids of last-ing love when we were
young on Butter-milk Hill. Yes I fought to win her love. The bat-tle that day I
lost, but won my true love. You've got to fight for love at all cost. We were
Chorus
best of friends all sum - mer long. And year af - ter year our love grew strong. Then
came the sum-mer of chance, some say a first ro-mance. We did in-tend to be best of
friends. We were best of friends all sum-mer long. And
Chorus
year af - ter year our love grew strong. Then came the sum-mer of chance, some say a

107
D G D
4
first ro - mance. We did in - tend to be best of
110
G D G
friends.

When I Turn, You Are Gone

Lyrics by
Richard Mousseau

Score by
Richard Mousseau

♩=92 Classic Country
Intro
Am Em Am D G Am C
V 1
Dreams of
7
D G D
you haunt my mem-or - y - . I can't seem to wake to face the day a -
13
G Em C Am D G
lone - . In my dreams I will hold you close - . Then you fade a -
19
D G Am C D
V 2
way, my heart is left to moan - . Each long day, my world is emp -
25
G D G Em C
ty - . I can't wait for sleep, to take me back to you - . Where in
31
Am D G D
dreams you and I em - brace - . Each time I whisp - er my love for you is

684 Walls Rd. Prince Twp., Ontario Canada P6A 6K4
mooseenterprises@on.aibn.com www.moosehidebooks.com

37 G Am Em D G 2
Chorus
true - . At times I feel your ess-ence, then my heart be-gins to yearn. I
42 Am Em Am D G Am
Bridge
sence your faint fra-grance. You are gone when I turn.
47 Em D G Am Em
52 Am D G Am Em D
Chorus
At times I feel your ess-ence, then my heart be-gins to
57 G Am Em Am D G Am C
V 2
yearn. I sence your faint fra-grance. You are gone when I turn. Each long
63 D G D
day, my world is emp - ty - . I can't wait for sleep, to take me back to
69 G Em C Am D G
you - . Where in dreams you and I em - brace-. Each time I whisp-
75 D G Am Em
Chorus
er my love for you is true - . At times I feel your ess-ence, then

80
D G Am Em
3
my heart be-gins to yearn. I sence your faint fra-grance. You are
84
Am D G Am D G
End
gone when I turn. When I turn you are gone.

When My Days Are Done

Lyrics by
Richard Mousseau

Score by
Richard Mousseau

♩=104 Classic Country/Western
Intro
G D Em
6 C V 1 G
When my days are done and the sun be-gins to set, I wish to lay on a
11 Em D
prair - ie mound to the sounds of a sweet du - et. As lone - ly dov - es
15 G
coo and prair-ie dogs chirp a soft good - night. I'll sleep with dreams of a life that will
20 D Em C V 2
fade with the morn-ing light. When my chores are done and the
24 G
herd be-gins to rest, I'll lay u - pon the prair - ie grass as the
28 Em D
sun goes to sleep in the west. I'll turn my best friend out for a job well

32
G
D
2
done, now free to roam. I'll sleep with hope that his life on the plains will be his
37
G
Chorus
home. When my days are done, u - pon the prair-ie grass I'll
41
C
D
sleep. A wrang-ler's life I've had, just my pals left to weep.
46
G
Am
D
My old hound with head u-pon my chest, with my last breath he knows I am at
51
G
Bridge
D
Em
rest.
56
C
V 3
G
When the sea-sons pass, I will be with my old friends. We'll ride the dus - ty
61
Em
D
cat - tle drives where the trails of the west nev-er end. I'll ride old Pa -
65
G
cos from dawn till dusk, all day we'll roam. To drift with time is my life and ride the

70
D G
Chorus
3
plains I call my home. When my days are done, u -
74
C
pon the prair-ie grass I'll sleep. A wrang-ler's life I've had, just my pals left to
79
D G Am
weep. My old hound with head u-pon my chest, with my last breath he
84
D G
End
knows I am at rest. When my days are done I will
88
D Em
rest.

Why Do You Love Me

Lyrics by
Richard Mousseau

Score by
Richard Mousseau

684 Walls Rd. Prince Twp., Ontario Canada P6A 6K4
mooseenterprises@on.aibn.com www.moosehidebooks.com

30
Em
lie. And this is the rea - son why. I don't do what guys do when
34
G
Am
wander-ing a-way from home. You're the on-ly one I love so back to you I'll al-ways
38
D
Daug
D6
Daug
D6
V 2
D
D♯
E
E♭
roam. Why do you love me ev - en though I treat you
42
D
D6
D
E
D
Daug
bad? Your friends warned you I'd take all the love you had then turn my
46
G
Am
A♭aug
D
G
back and walk a - way, but now I have some-thing to say. I've
50
Em
been a fool from the start, each time I've hurt your heart. When I for -
54
G
Am
get your birth-day or lose you down at the mall. I nev-er do honey-do
58
D
G
chores and that ain`t all. But hon-ey this ain`t no lie. And this is the rea-son

63
Em
G
3
why. I don't do what guys do when wander-ing a-way from home. You're the
67
Am
D
Daug D6
Daug D6
Bridge
D
on-ly one I love so back to you I'll al-ways roam.
71
D♯
E
E♭
D
D6
D
E
76
D
Daug G
Am
A♭aug D
Daug D6
Daug D6
V 3
D
Why do you love
81
D♯
E
E♭
D
D6
D
E
me ev-en though I treat you bad? Your friends warned you I'd take all the love you
86
D
Daug G
Am
A♭aug D
G
had then turn my back and walk a - way, but now I have some-thing to say. My
91
G
Em
hon-ey I'll nev - er lie. And this is the rea - son why. I've
95
G
Em
been your fool from the start, I love you with all my heart. I've

99
G
4
been your fool from the start, I love you with all my heart

You Brought Me Down

Lyrics by
Richard Mousseau

Score by
Richard Mousseau

=116 Rock
Intro
Gm
C
D
Gm
V 1
You brought me down
C
with words in town, spread-ing all your lies to make my moth-er
D
Gm
cry. You brought me down,
V 2
word got a - round
C
D
Gm
that I did cheat with a gal on the street. You brought me
Chorus
C
Gm
down with your lie. I don't know why you brought me down.

684 Walls Rd. Prince Twp., Ontario Canada P6A 6K4
mooseenterprises@on.aibn.com www.moosehidebooks.com

34
C
Gm
2
38
C
42
D
Gm
Chorus
You brought me down with your
46
C
Gm
C
lie. I don't know why you brought me down.
51
Gm
V 3
You brought me down, your lies will nev-er set you free. Do your
56
Em
C
D
Gm
pet-ty ways bring you glee to bring me down? You brought me
61
V 4
Em
C
down. One day soon the table will turn and the pain of sor-row you will learn
66
D
Gm
V 5
when you're brought down. You'll be brought down

70
C
3
when the truth gets round. it's your turn to cry and that's no
75
D
Gm
End
lie. You'll be brought down.
79
C
83
D
Gm
87
C
90
D
Gm

You Have To Win

Lyrics by
Richard Mousseau

Score by
Richard Mousseau

♩=116 Classic Country
Intro
V 1
It's just a game - you have to win - . Ev-ery-one knows - of your sin - . And why you cheat - - the count-less men - . It's just a game of love you have to win - . They say that
Chorus 1
you - col - lect wed-ding rings - , so am I just - - an-oth - er fling - ? The hearts you break - - by self - ish sin - - to you it's just a game you have to win.
Bridge

684 Walls Rd. Prince Twp., Ontario Canada P6A 6K4
mooseenterprises@on.aibn.com www.moosehidebooks.com

V 2
The next in line - - I pit-ty him - . Like all be-fore -
, love's vic-tims - , you tease with love - - then give pois-on -
. To you it's just a game you have to win - . You tease with love be-
Chorus 2
hind a greed-y grin - . To you it's just - - a game to win -
. One day you'll lose - - love's vic-tim - . then you will know just
how it feels - , yes how it feels - not to win.
Nc

www.ingramcontent.com/pod-product-compliance
Lightning Source LLC
Chambersburg PA
CBHW081234090426
42738CB00016B/3298
* 9 7 8 1 9 2 7 3 9 3 7 9 6 *